ANO HOTEL ROOM

Selected Poems 1988-2008

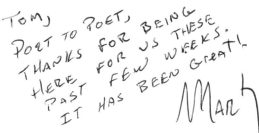

Steven Marty Grant

Edited by Ruth Walters

Another Hotel Room
Copyright © 1988, 1989, 1990, 1999, 2000, 2001, 2007, 2008 by
Steven Marty Grant
Grace Notes Books, Ventura Ca 93004

Cover Photo by Hollye-Faye
Cover Design by Harmoni McGlothlin

All rights reserved.
Materials published in this book are the intellectual property of the author and Grace Notes Books. Any reproduction of these materials (except in the case of brief quotations embodied in critical articles and reviews) must be done only with consent of the publisher and author. For Permission information please contact via email at permissions@gracenotesbooks.com or write to 10254 Alexandria St., Ventura Ca 93004.

First Printing US October, 2008

**2nd US Printing 2011 Another Hotel Room (Special Edition)
Published by Grace Notes Books**

ISBN #9781463696436

LIBRARY OF CONGRESS CATALOGING IN PUBLICATION DATA

Grant, Steven Marty.
    Another Hotel Room

ACKNOWLEDGEMENT

I want to thank the people in my life that have encouraged me to pursue my love of poetry and the written word: Phyllis Grant, Claudia Basha, Carol Golliher, Melissa Olsen, Dave Elzie and all my friends and fellow writers at TIBU. I want to say a special thank you to my beautiful and patient wife Susan. Grateful acknowledgement is also given to the following magazines and websites where some of these poems originally appeared: The Writer, Spring Harvest, VVC Drama & English Journal, www.notesandgracenotes.com, www.thisisby.us, www.greatwriting.co.uk, and www.wildpoetryforum.com.

For
Susan, Taylor, Nelda and Phyllis,
without their love my life would be a lot less meaningful.

TABLE OF CONTENTS

6	Foreword

The Road Suite (1997)

12	North Minneapolis, Saturday Night 10:30 PM
13	Still in Minneapolis
14	Another Hotel Room
15	The Night I Fucked Loneliness
16	Choosing
17	Drinking
18	Slow Learner

Selected Poems (1988 – 2008)

20	Search for Comparison
21	ee Bukowski
22	Daddy's Girl
23	Me v You
24	Dropped
25	A Prayer
26	Lost Forever
27	Roses & Reflections
28	Booze
29	All-A-Board
30	Love Drunk
31	Wasted Youth
32	Time
33	Since There Was You
34	Sunset at Trestles
35	Solstice to Equinox
36	Late Fees
37	End Jamb
38	Inside Joke
39	The Day Before
40	Happenstance
41	Communication Terminated
42	A Different Tune
43	Desire
44	Tryst
45	Paramour
46	Scars in the Afterglow
47	Taken Back
48	Incomplete Heart
49	Tits & Guns
50	The Color
51	Night Rise
52	Raid!

53	Pretentious Little Poet by the Poetry Rack at Borders
54	Walk
55	I Do
56	Man
57	Tattoos
58	Quiet
59	Tomorrow Never Comes
60	Pavlovian

A Year in New York (2007-2008)

62	Inspiration
63	Cutting
64	Beneath the Rose
65	Click Clique Cliché
66	Internet Porn
67	Write Blocked
68	Codeine Tequila & Beer
69	Manahachtanienk
70	Urbanality
71	Union Square
72	*"I opened myself up to the gentle indifference"*
73	Screw You Walt Whitman
74	Lycaon of the Lower East Side
75	Letters to the Editor
77	Doldrums
78	Fall of New York
79	Out of Chaos
80	La Cantera
81	Insomnia
82	Simplicity
83	Poet Warrior
84	The Weight of My Own Self Importance
85	**Bonus Poem:** Sad Girl on an Uptown Train
86	**Bonus Poem:** 9 to 5 Icarus
87	**Bonus Poem:** Eastern Terminus
88	**Author Q&A**
92	The Folks Who Made It Happen

FOREWORD
by Harmoni McGlothlin

Steven Grant describes himself as "A Southern California boy lost in Manhattan." His work mirrors this description at every turn, reminiscent of both the pulsing grit of Gotham and the crashing of Pacific waves against a timeless mountainside.

With the squalor of the city looming; his words make the heart ache for the loneliness and the stench, the noise and the chaos with lines like:

> *A week ago,*
> *I was a stick of butter*
> *greasing 23rd Street*

Countering the hopelessness of this, he then paints a picture in emotion that becomes a slow dance, growing and blossoming. Grant beckons the reader to melt into his imagery and become a part of it. The music flows flawlessly in "Lost Forever":

> *"As light slowly*
> *pries loose the last*
> *fingers of night*
> *clinging to the landscape,*
> *the shine of innocence*
> *appears tarnished and tired."*

In turn, reality being a constant antagonist to this poet's pen, he jolts the reader, saying:

> *"Fantasy, bliss and bullshit*

feed infatuation"

and rips the spleen out of romance with this stanza:

> *"Every orgasm*
> *a butcher's cleaver*
> *separating bone*
> *from sinew"*

The balance of Steven's works, harsh yet gentle, hopeful yet futile, is what truly separates him from the hordes of New York poets crowding the sadness-stained sidewalks of the city. He transcends cliché and sparks new meaning in the phrase "poetic device".

"It's so easy to be a poet
and so hard to be a man."
-Charles Bukowski

The Road Suite
(1997)

North Minneapolis, Saturday Night, 10:30 pm

I've spent over
two hours
reading poetry books
and drinking
effeminate
overpriced coffee.

The bookstore is full
of tattooed geeks,
lesbians
erudite intellectuals
and me.

The place
is supposed to close
at eleven
so the clerk
anxiously
watches us,
as we dirty the pages.

We all just sit,
and read
and wait,
to be tossed out.

I am pretty sure
that each and every
one of us would
trade all of these
wonderful books

for a date.

Still in Minneapolis

Saturday
snuck up on me
like I was a fly
and it was a swatter.
Does this every week
when I'm on the road.
Monday through Friday
I can bury my loneliness
beneath all the work
I have to do, then suddenly
I'm smashed up against the wall,
blood and guts running
all the way to Sunday afternoon.
The weekend becomes
an endless, loveless,
marathon of hours
to be endured and survived.
The lighthouse beacon
of Monday morning
beckons me to shore,
a shinning illusion
of hope.

Another Hotel Room

Four and half months on the road
and loneliness finally caught me.
Stole into my room,
sat at the foot of my bed
and shook me from a fitful sleep.
Her cold stethoscope touch
pulled what remained of my self respect
out through my chest into the night air.
When the panic wore off
I fell back to sleep at peace,
comforted that at least she
would never leave me.

The Night I Fucked Loneliness

Stalked me
for years
every bar
every town

She was there

Beyond sight
without touch
nightly waking
sound of nothing

She was there

late again
one more night
Johnny Walker
self pity rocks
waiting for me
the emptiness
dark room
another hotel

She was there

Giving in
I embraced her

Choosing

...after a while
I started fucking
my way back,
to sanity
and self respect.
Pining away
just seemed
so pathetic
and pointless.

Every orgasm
a butcher's cleaver
separating bone
from sinew,
ripping me away
from what I clung to,
tearing me
from you.

Decay would achieve
the same end,
it would just take
more patience,
more endurance.
Waiting might
be less drastic
but it would be
a lot more pitiful
and painful.

Drinking

At one point I thought
I could drink myself into oblivion,
kill myself, one shot at a time.
Whiskey was the journey,
intoxication the destination.
Alcohol, like blood
that coursed through my pain,
fed it, nurtured it,
an orphan child
held by a dispassionate nun.

I learned to live with the knowledge
that pain, like death, was inevitable
well beyond my control
only to be quelled, never cured.
Drunkenness however
was completely in my control;
like a lion on a leash,
or a fire built to warm
my house of straw.

Slow Learner

I hate mornings after!
My mouth tastes
like a Manhattan
sidewalk
and my head
throbs with
every beat of my heart.
Mornings after
are a time
for inventory,
counting and recounting
the drunkenness, debauchery,
and stupidity
that define
my social life.
Mornings after
smell of spilled booze,
stale cigarettes,
and the perfume
of cheap bar girls
passed out in the bedroom.
Mornings after
sting like a ruler
across the knuckles,
wielded by
Sister Barely Tolerant,
correcting me in ethics class.
Mornings after
serve as a harsh reminder
of what excess can lead to.
Somehow those lessons
never come to mind
on nights before.

**Selected Poems
(1988-2008)**

Search for Comparison

I can't find a metaphor
for life, love, hate or death,
a cab in the Manhattan rain,
or a cresting wave in Kansas.

I desperately need a metaphor
for lies and truths, wants and wishes,
a star for navigation through the night,
a thunderstorm on a sun parched face.

Tonight I crave a metaphor
for God and angels, for heaven or the cross,
like a starving man at a kitchen window
drooling over others' food in vain.

I haven't any left, no metaphors
no joy, only sadness, abandoned by my muse,
a fish flopping aimlessly in the sand,
a sorrowful dog standing on a country road.

ee Bukowski

I pick-
ed
      up
thisextordinarywoman
(at
the track)

She
was new
toall
      this bet
ting   the ponies
      shit
and so (by
the
way)
impressed she was
with my
            prowess
that
      she
gave me
         allofher

money which I
lost
as quick
ly
as
I had
my own

Daddy's Girl

Small feet running;
tears, so many tears
   "it's broken"

Knowing look comforts;
patience and glue
   "thank you daddy"

Little girl laughing;
giggles, screams and giggles
   "catch me"

Steady hands toss;
catching, gently catching
   "again again"

Tiny ears covering;
shouts angry shouts
   "stop please stop"

Somber judge intones;
Mom vs. Dad
   "for the petitioner"

Deep voice explaining;
fault, not your fault
   "mommy and daddy…"

Small hands cling;
sobs, guttural sobs
   "come home daddy"

Desperate kisses and hugs;
visitation, odd weekends
   "I can't baby"

Big feet running;
tears, so many tears
   "it's broken"

Me v You

When human frailty
goes from metaphor
to emergency; words
are inadequate bandages.

The visceral urgency
of bone protruding through skin
is such simple beauty.
A reduction, a stitch or 12,
a few feet of gauze and tape
and it will be all right in a week or two.

When human bonds
go from till death
to divorce court, "pain"
is an inadequate word.

The affecting wound
of forever becoming nevermore
is such exquisite agony.
A separation, a lawyer or two,
a few hours in family court
and nothing will ever be quite right again.

Dropped

My heart:
A puzzle
spilled
from its box,
several pieces
missing.

Thought
for a time you
had taken them.
Upon rethinking
know, they were
always missing.

I'd used
pieces of you
to fill the gaps,
your pieces
covered holes,
but never
did fill them.

A Prayer

God make me young again,
let the cynicism of my years
disappear, make the bitter
taste of my failings turn
to sugar in my mouth.

Fill me again
with the faith of my youth,
mending each scar time
has etched on my heart.
Help me to love
without fear of
pain, loss or boredom.

Revive the well
of my tears, dry these many
years, touch my eyes
with spit and dirt,
wash away the darkness
and let me see you.

Lost Forever

At sunrise
God breathes
fire and smoke
into azure morning,
as the demiurge groans
back into motion.

Last night
the world stopped,
dreams and motivations
became paper icons
engulfed in pyre flashes;
Ashes to ashes

As light slowly
pries loose the last
fingers of night
clinging to the landscape,
the shine of innocence
appears tarnished and tired.

Last night
a hero became mortal
human, uncoiled,
glint of his armor
dulled with rust;
dust to dust

The midday sun
hangs, half mast
in the horizon,
weakly illuminating
yet another void;
a diminished world.

Last night
God blinked,
in that omni-second,
the words fell silent,
inspiration stolen;
Amen

Roses & Reflections

Today I am thinking of that little gazebo,
where we stood under a canopy of white roses.
We vowed with tear-stained cheeks,
and promised to trust and love eternal.

Memories drift back and pause next to you
on the shore of that pond up state.
I can almost hear your gentle laughter
as I stroke your cheek with that yellow rose bud.

I recall Sunday mornings beneath
our old comforter, patterned with faded roses.
We shared the confidence of well worn lovers
with little left to prove.

This mourning, as I stand in the rain
admiring your decorated grave,
I know that I will carry this love sub rosa;
in secret until we are together again.

Booze

Oh
to worship
at the altar
of drunken
abandon.

Confess
your sins,
and revel
in liquid
Absolut(ion).

There
is salvation
in intoxication,
for I am 10 feet tall
at 100 proof!

All-a-board

She loved
being in love
the danger
the possibility
of total defeat

Moved from
train wreck
to train wreck
never
contemplating
alternative
transportation

When she
boarded me
I quickly
switched
to a dead end
track

Guess
we all crave
the sensation
of steel
entangling
and grinding
to a horrible
stop

Love Drunk

The epiphany:

Infatuation
brilliant flash,
confusion followed
by dazed
emotional intoxication.

Self... serving,
feeding,
absorbed,
deluded.

No regard, for reality

Fuck Reality!

Reality washes the dishes
every night, mows the lawn
and never remembers
to put the seat down.

Fantasy, bliss and bullshit
feed infatuation.

Idealized romantic dreams,
whispering words of seduction,
and blowing kisses in the dark.
Doesn't have bills to pay,
never watches TV,
and is always
in the mood.

Emotional intemperance,
love hangover:

Repeat as necessary.

Wasted Youth

2 am used to feel
like the edge of life
and beer was the blood
that made it possible.
Back in the day
when screaming at the world
was a sacred right
and night was its temple,
the future was a minefield
and the past did not exist.
Love was like salvation,
the arms of a lover heaven.
Death lived in middle earth
eternal life behind the wheel.
A glorious summer day was truth
Hot August Night a record.
Life had a clarity too pure to question
and the moon still followed me at night.

God, I miss 18!

I have found myself longing to return
to the days of my self discovery,
when I could revel in my freedom
and crow at the stark desert night.
Unaware that I was at once,
master and slave of my universe,
asleep under a black canopy
riddled with the moth holes of age,
oblivious to the shortness of my days
and the length of my reach.

Time

Tic...Tic...Tic...

The lunatic marches
pushing in the edges of immortality
closing the doors of forever

Tic...Tic...Tic...

He is coming closer
Rhythmatic
Systematic
Death

Tic...

Since There Was You

I never held your hand,
didn't taste the sweet
and salty joy of your lips,
or pull you close enough
to feel your every breath.

We never stood on the edge
of sacred night to watch
the world fall into sunsets sleep,
never consecrated the sand
on an abandoned beach.

I never saw you drift off
in the dim of the moon,
never wished on a star's falling,
or chased away the evening chill
with my arms around you.

We have passed our days
with a subtle smile,
an engaging glance,
and I was left to dream
of what could not be.

But since there was you,
the desert inside my chest
has finally tasted rain.
The beacon of ever after
burns brighter on the horizon.

Sunset at Trestles

Daylight danced
with lengthening shadows
along the strand
as night pushed
slowly down
toward the horizon.

Eight hours
of waves and sun
had washed away
the work week, and
we collapsed in sandy piles
of smiles and salty skin.

Driftwood smoke
mingled with
misty sea air,
the sun teased,
then fell into
a waiting ocean.

I kissed you
for the first time,
and when the moon
winked from the East,
I thought that we
might fall in love.

The fire burned down to embers.

I searched for wood to stoke it.

Solstice to Equinox

Anaïs, Anaïs;
Litha has passed
and we are left
to mourn the coming
autumnal balance, for
creatures such as we
crave the severe
and eschew
this gentle world.

Travel with me to
The Tropic of Capricorn
and leave behind
the ever shrinking
days of Cancer.
There we can live
in eternal summer
and Black Spring.

Grieve not my love,
for with the arrival
of Yoole's long nights,
Sirius shall align
with Orion's belt
and point us back
to the elliptical
apex, and June.

Late Fees

I know you watch me,
over spectacle rims
near the bridge's end.

You shush me
over index cards
and collected late fees.

I want to tie you up
or hold you down
and scribble poems
on your breasts
in red fountain pen
and let your screams
echo through
the Dewey stacks.

We both know
pain and love
are partners
over time, overdue.

End Jamb

The conversation was rife
with well timed
pauses; intended
to keep balance at
bay. I raised my glass, sipped
slowly--deliberately.

"We really need to
talk" echoed over
the tinkle of
glass and silver
night.

"Maybe some time" // "apart"

(caesura)

The evening's exchange wore down, then end-stopped.

Inside Joke

A phone rings in the darkness
of a Tuesday night and I
raise my glass and whisper,
"please leave a message at the tone."

I am chasing heart failure in bathtub
or aspirated vomit on a hotel toilet,
but I might be a few corrosives short.

The footsteps outside my window
continue to come and go, but they
only motivate me to turn up the radio
and crack another tax stamp.

You told me once that all things
have a beginning as well as an end,
and I laughed at your pessimism.

As I sit here alone on the crest
of Wednesday morning crash
I can't remember why
I thought that was funny.

The Day Before;

when we were still
necessary. Conversations
thoughtfully avoided
unpleasant topics.

when I still loved
the fairytale. Endings
that I never saw
in tomorrows light.

when you still thought
I was the one. Man,
what a difference
in 24 hours of life.

Happenstance

Love died today
didn't make headlines
happens all the time

Like a drive-by
poor bastard
laying in a pool
of his own heartbreak

MAC-10
somebody's hurt
somebody's gone
love is dead

Just happens like that
except nothing
really just happens...

Communication Terminated

In the dim candlelight
of romantic deceptions,
she served me my soul
with rice and beans,
fed me my insensitivity
and poured a tall glass of shame
to help me wash it down.
I said that I did not mean to;
she asked "then why did you?"
I said I only wanted to;
she snapped "then why didn't you?"
When I finished the last bite
of my own cruelty,
she smirked "are you ready for pie?"
I declined,
quite full of myself.

A Different Tune

I
  fell
      in
          love
with Jazz
intoxicating rhythm
without
rhyme or reason
                          random
patterns
          and
dangerous curves
I've always loved music
but Jazz
was the first music
that loved me back
her eyes
captivate
and penetrate
she plays
          in my mind
and plays
          with my emotions
caresses my ears
dances on my lips
and
     fucks me
               like a Bangkok whore
she rips my heart
from my chest
and
     squeezes it
              to her own
                       peculiar beat

Desire

I long
for you,
ache, barely
able to breath
in your absence.

Innocent and seductive,
worldly and childlike.
I lie awake and dream
of your taste,
your texture,
I can almost feel
each delicate freckle
of your back,
as I envelope you
in my arms.
I crave your lips,
your touch,
the pounding wave
of your tongue
crashing voraciously
into mine.

I am starving
without you,
I hate myself
for needing you,
for feeling lost
empty, pointless
and weak
with you
gone.

Tryst

"I was hoping I would see you again",
the words danced on my ear,
her breath and breasts warm against me,
"so I didn't wear panties".
Outwardly unaffected,
I leaned in to take the fragrance
of her hair as it floated past my nose.
My lips pressed against her ear,
I made it known, I was pleased as well.
Her hand fell to my knee
and slid deliberately north.
"So it would seem", she said
with a firm and knowing grasp.
The bar was crowded when I entered,
but as she slid her lithe frame
between the bar and my stool,
everything peripheral faded from focus.

"You ran away last time before I finished with you"
My explanations quickly rebuffed,
she kissed me.
My James Bond countenance began to crack.
"Now that wasn't so hard was it?"
she giggled, and came back for seconds.
She pulled me closer
positioning my hands on her waist.
I know there was loud music playing
but all I could hear was the sound of her voice as she said
"do you know how wet you're making me?"
With a deft fluid motion, she slid my hand down
and back up under the hem of her skirt,
removing any thought
that she was prone to exaggeration.
I caught my breath,
regained my composure,
looked past her coolly, and made it known
I was ready to close out my tab.

Paramour

Angel of night
she delights,
sweet taste; fruit forbidden.

Fall from grace
I embrace,
Wider path; down she leads.

Immortal cost,
salvation lost,
sublime seduction; apple bitten.

Life of sin,
accept/begin,
restive desire; lust she feeds.

Scars in the Afterglow

Her skin still glistened wet,
with the remnants of ecstasy.
I, with the gentlest touch,
began to trace the scars
on her back with my fingers.
Slowly she drifted off
as I kissed her shoulder.
I savored the saltiness on my lips
and her scent filled my senses.
The motion of time gave way to stillness
as I continued to trace the scars.
She woke, and with a sad smile sighed,
"so that is how it's supposed to be."
She dressed quickly,
seductive red satin falling
delicately over the cicatrix maze
that was forever etched in my mind.

Taken Back

There is a song
that plays
in my head
soundtrack
to my
transgressions

The melody
gently washes
over me
in rhythmic
waves of guilt
and pleasure

Each crescendo
a musical
climax shaking
my memory
and breaking
my resolve

Words of betrayal
that echo
my regret
lyrical
condemnations
each of my
missteps

There is a song
replaying
in my mind
background
on the radio
the night
it all went wrong

Incomplete Heart

October evening
some years ago,
by chance we met
and came to know,
animal passion
so seldom felt,
gnawing desire
and crippling regret.

Backwards look
that crazy time,
touched your heart,
gave pieces of mine,
you still have them
and always will,
no fairytale ending
but I long for you
still.

Tits & Guns

Isolated
on this
crowded avenue,
in this land
of violent anarchy,
where the ignorant
are governed
by the intimidating,
I am no more
than a bourgeois
Caucasian tourist.

On these streets
pious intellectualism
is but a dog
pissing on a hydrant
philosophy, sociology
and psychology all run,
tails between their legs,
at the first bark
of a 9mm pit bull.

This is rule
by the work-less class
in an inverse universe.
Representative whores,
thugs and junkies
lobby for power,
cash and crack.
Tits and Guns
are electoral votes
in the primary
of survival.

The Color

The color of death,
seen on the face of age,
shows up in the street,
worn and tired
pushing a shopping cart.
Death's color
tints the air
from the third world
to the cities of the West,
looking like
a starving child,
or a glass vial.
The color of death
stains the hands
of corporate America,
selling opium, cocaine,
and acid
in thirty second segments
of prime time.
Death's color,
not of the spectrum,
is visible
in the heart and mind.
Lust for power,
avarice,
rage, hate and fear
blend
and become one;
one belief,
one goal,
one color.

Night Rise

The night rises
to the sound of a baby crying
alone in a garbage can.
The air,
thick with the noise
of cars and gunfire,
smells of rot and Burger King.
The city streets whisper
words of seduction
to lonely old men
seeking companionship
at a price.
The sign on a bar
preaches a neon gospel;
OPEN 'TIL 4AM
OPEN 'TIL 4AM
to those
in need of escape.
In the heart
a church,
doors locked, windows barred,
stands separate
from the pain.
With the dawn
comes sleep for the darkness,
until the world
turns its face away again.

Raid!

Opportunity
knocks gently,
in the afternoon.
Responsibility
kicks down the door
at midnight,
and pulls you
screaming
from your
peace of mind.

Pretentious Little Poet by the Poetry Rack at Borders

"If you like Bukowski
then you should
definitely
check out
this anthology.
It has several
*of **my** poems*
in it and
Bukowski
is my
biggest
influence."

Walk

The day
is wrinkled
and worn
like Saturday
evening's dress
on Sunday
morning.

Don't worry
sweetheart
the city
won't tell
your mother,
and neither
will I.

I Do

In the end
I began
after all
was said
I was
done
in
the beginning
I died only
to live again
and again
with the
rebirth
of death
do us part.

Man

Humanity's tripped
and can't seem to get up.

Exactly what caused the stumble,
I couldn't say,
but to this day
he sits there holding his foot
bemoaning his condition.

According to some
he was chewing gum
and walking,
that's what got him.

At any rate he's not talking.

Tattoos

Mary Jane
Never Quit

I Handle Snakes
In Country '68
Stairway to Heaven

I Love my Mother
Only on a Harley
Long May She Wave
for God & Country

Quiet

To sit
unmoving
requires
an indulgence
not often found.
In this age
of mindless motion
it is truly rare
to see
with closed eye
but open mind,
the true beauty
of God
and his creation
to listen to a voice
not easily heard
for it has
no sound.

Tomorrow Never Comes

We tell each
other lies
under covers
of darkness,
eternal love,
conjoined
broken hearts.

We savor
the night
rapt
in your sheets,
and feed
on passion,
bare flesh,
heartbeats.

I could
give myself,
but no,
because
I know
you won't
love me
tomorrow.

Lifetime of
yesterdays,
eternal tonight,
because
you know
that I won't
love you
tomorrow.

Pavlovian

It had been
six months
and the blue
in her eyes
still burned
brighter than June's
mid-day sky.

I had expected
the hunger
to be gone,
but when I saw her,
the bells
began to ring,
and I was
immediately
ravenous.

I longed
to satiate myself
in her arms,
to devour her,
drink in her soul
and gorge myself
on the radiance
of her smile.

A Year in New York
(2007-2008)

Inspiration

I spend Sunday afternoons
in Greenwich Village
searching for Holden
and old Sal Paradise.
I want to connect
with the dissonance ,
embrace madness
and take On the Road.

I stutter step 42nd Street,
weave and eaves drop
on stolen conversations
and snap shot scenes.
Sublime brief glimpses,
of a television set to scan.
Seen through dim glass
a city viewed darkly.

I've fucked my share
of whores and goddesses
but I still can't write
a decent love poem.
Language fails compared
to the splendor and stench
of two becoming one,
then two, or maybe none.

I walk through Central Park
and wonder about the ducks,
I often take the time to ask
the junkies "where's Dean?"
and every once in a while
they give me a knowing look
and say "he's on the journey,
living it, where are you man?"

Cutting

A razor's edge glides
through dermis
with a surgeon's
disconnected precision.

Crimson tattooed
parallel lines
concealed for now
on the inner thigh.

Ejaculated blood spatters;
a decorative memento
for the bathroom floor.

Endorphins engage
serotonin orgasms,
and the impulse wanes
while platelets seek
companionship.

Tonight she will sleep,
tomorrow's hungry voice
but a whisper that will grow
in the darkness.

Beneath the Rose

Meet me
under cover(s)
in clandestine
destinations,
trust betrayal,
lust and fate
to Harpocrates
discretion.

Beneath
crimson petals,
we can sate
carnal appetites,
well beyond
prying eyes,
our secrets safe
beneath the rose.

Meet me
in our holy place
and confess
your dark wishes.
Let us do
the unspeakable
shielded by
the gift of Eros.

I will hold you
and whisper
"Sub rosa,
my secret love".
For we are gods
and our deeds,
cannot be judged
by mortals.

Click Clique Cliché

Right, left, double and drag
or is it cylinder and hammer?
Perhaps a door latch closing;
only the potential for pain
makes it a scary sound.

A group of individuals
(including you, excluding me)
which is used as a standard by which
to (speciously) evaluate
attitudes (clothes),
abilities (looks),
or current situations (money).
As a reference group it can be
either normative (oppressive)
or comparative (judgmental).

With every fiber of my being,
I long to be with you again.
My heart aches and my soul cries out,
for I am nothing without you.

Left click drag,
highlight,
right click,
delete.

Hammer cock/
Cylinder rotate

Internet Porn

Power on
(thump thump)
boot up
(thump thump)
0-ICU-812
enter
click/click
(thump thump)
http://www.herm-aphrodite.com
enter

Streaming
video connections
and tumescent
blue screen love

Grip and click
unzip re-grip
mouse pad palm sweat
rhythm and beat

repeat

repeat

Write Blocked

The white screen
taunts me with
a cursor's wink
while I drill holes
in my skull
in search of gold.

Twenty six
alpha bitches
make promises,
ask for shape
and definition;
instructions
not included.

I feel like
a middle class
needle romancer,
cruising Hunts Point,
in search of my next
opium love affair.

Thalia smiles
and assures me
that I hold the keys,
then giggles and winks
when I ask her
"to which door?"

Codeine, Tequila & Beer

Bitter pills go down
easier with a beer chaser
so I am avoiding
cracks in the sidewalk
and warning labels.

God made tequila
so that mortals could
know what he feels like
on Sundays and Mondays
during football season.

Pain and codeine
are like movie violence
but only if my wife
lets me hold the remote
and we eat in front of the TV.

Learning from your mistakes
is about as useful as unzipping
after your pants are wet
or buckling up after the bone
protrudes through bloody skin.

Drug addicts, trauma victims
and poets spend too much
time in the company
of their own complaining
about being misunderstood.

Twist off bottle caps
are for people
with two good hands
but pop-top cans
don't discriminate.

It's dark now but I can see
well enough to know I am
on the floor, I've spilled my drink
and that child proof
may be an understatement.

Manahachtanienk
"Place of general inebriation"

Henry's boys
on the Halve Maen
must have seen
something in 1609,
sliding up river,
mapping future
condo projects
up and down
the Hudson.
For 400 years,
disappointment
has left its mark
on this city, ground
into the pavement
by centuries
of footsteps
up and down
the avenues.
Concentration
8 hours at a time,
57th to Wall Street,
Standard &
Poor Sobibór
as trains carry
their daily load
up and down
the tracks.
The lure
of Goldman
Sachs logic, so
we keep coming,
as fortunes rise
and humans fall
like marquee names
up and down
Broadway.

Urbanality

I was never one to write about sunsets or birds,
to be honest that shit bores me to distraction.
I live in Manhattan so I haven't seen a sunset
in three hundred & sixty five days, and birds here,
well they're just another pest to be controlled.
I never really liked to listen to sweet ballads
and there's something pathetic about the blues.
I prefer the hard rocking sounds of Hindi profanity
sung by cab drivers, the tune of droning car horns
and the distant wail of another siren's song of ending.
I never got much pleasure from hiking or picnics
and I have no real desire to get back to nature.
I'd rather choke down a cart hot dog for breakfast,
avoid piss puddles on the subway platform
and hide behind Ray-Bans and an eighty gig iPod.
I never understood the fascination with beauty
or people' neurotic obsession with falling in love.
I've seen a lot of well groomed hair and make up jobs
and have had the shit kicked out of me more than once,
but beauty is a rocks glass, love is a generous bartender,
and the poetry is between the first sip and "hit me again".

Union Square

A bum recites
absurdist poetry
to passers by
and collects change
in a fake Burberry cap
while I slowly sip
my Sunday morning
and shop for open air
jalapeños, mushrooms
and cilantro.

Paint-bucket drummers
provide a steady back beat
as weekend consumers
are called to worship
and the church crowd
is released from servitude.

Across the square
a painter discusses politics
with a jewelry maker
and a guy in a Gumby t-shirt.

The sun plays peek-a-boo
between the buildings
and I wonder how long
the fresh roses would last
if I decided to splurge.

A toddler pilots a stroller
down the sidewalk
parents in tow
while four teens
knee and kick
a Hacky Sack
back and forth.

These are the moments
when the city speaks to me
tells me four hundred year old
ghost stories and reminds me
that I am not alone.

***"I opened myself to the gentle
indifference of the world"***

They tried to make me feel different
like I wasn't connected or in touch,
but isn't everyone just doing time,
standing vigil and mourning without tears.

Eventually we all join this funeral procession,
a slow march through the scorching sun.
Conviction, condemnation and reprisal
are my rewards for calling the ritual absurd.

Some days I can imagine the crowd
shouting from the subway platform
as my train pulls away into the darkness,
cries of *"die Meursault die"* echoing down the line.

I can't really explain the four extra shots,
seemed like the thing to do at the time.
I have taken to wearing sunglasses,
that should be enough to show regret.

Screw You Walt Whitman!

Obscurity and irrelevance
are scarier than death,
so I write to leave my mark,
but I am writing in chalk
on the sidewalk of 7th Avenue
and 42nd Street. Tomorrow
my words will be washed away
by fashion footwear
and afternoon thunderstorms.

My fears breed behind decorated walls
and seem to be immune to bug spray,
but I can still chase them
out of the living room
when I turn on the lights.
I have no philosophy
that explains the nature of man,
and my lexicon is the product
of a public school education.
All I have to work with is Silly String,
Paint by Numbers pictures
and an old Poetry Writers Guide
picked up at a yard sale in Queens.

I have Body Electric nightmares,
and Walt Whitman keeps hitting
on Jim Morrison while he plays
the piano at Rick's Café Américain.
Despite my efforts the hairy bastard
won't even look in my direction.

Lycaon of the Lower East Side

Full moon Friday calls:
The promise of night
cloaks the travertine
and glass temples of man.
Silhouettes shape-shift
beyond streetlight glare
and gather in the shadows.
I am the seventh son;
dark ruler of alphabet city,
hungry in the lunar phase.

Satisfaction struts
in 4 inch heels
down Bleecker Street,
Chanel marinade
follows the footfall.
I watch with amber eye
and hold my tongue
behind eager teeth.

Tonight she will be my love,
and I will finally sleep--
safe from Aconitum dawn.

Letters to the Editor

I sat at my usual stool at the bar
and ignored the bartender's scowl.
"Yes those eight quarters are your fucking tip"
I thought without a moment of guilt.
Now that football season is over,
I find Sundays are best spent drinking and reading.
I refuse to jump on the machine
that is New York on any given weekend.
This city has no use for the disengaged,
or the conscientious objector, but I don't give a shit,
so I hide in dim corners until nightfall.

I was avoiding the sun and working
my way through a bottle of decent single malt
with an uppity west-side literary rag chaser.
I get a copy in the mail every time
they print one of my poems so vanity
forces me to at least give it the once over.
It was filled with everything you'd expect,
two pieces of short fiction, one pretty good
and the other not great, but a good story none the less.
Two dozen poems of various length and skill,
covering everything from love to Iraq and back again.
The Letters to the Editor were the usual prattle
bemoaning the dearth of true art in Western society.
One letter made it quite clear that sentimental crap
was unwelcome and pleased nobody.
Another, written by a grumpy little man,
railed against every poem (all of them) that did not
meet his educated discriminating standards.
As I read his editorial, I could picture the smirk spread
across his face. His little diatribe against the unworthy
amongst these pages, penned with great concern
for future generations of poetry readers everywhere.

A glance at my watch confirmed my suspicion

that the angry yellow sun should have mellowed a bit,
so I snatched half the change off the bar and walked out.
On my way home I gave the change and the magazine
to a homeless woman who thanked me with a blessing.
When I got back to my door I paused just long enough
to watch the remnants of tangerine melt into the Hudson,
and I smiled as I imagined the coming night.
There was poetry to be seen on the faces of the city
and in the single blade of grass pushing defiantly
through the Lexington Avenue sidewalk.

Doldrums

July rains
baptize garbage piles
on 26th street
then evaporate
to twilight steam.

September's still
beyond the horizon,
the soft shores of Spring
a distant dream
in my wake.

The Doldrums
of Gotham Summer
have becalmed my ship:
I am adrift
on a graffiti sea.

Adorned in albatross,
I will navigate
august Manhattan's
burning quiescence
and trade for Fall.

Fall of New York

Fifth Avenue:
Umbrellas bob
down the sidewalk
like drunken
Chinese lanterns
and a cool wind
has invaded in
from the north.

Summer's anger
still seethes
below street level
but today refused
to bare its teeth,
opting to stay dry
in the warm refuge
of the train tunnels.

A week ago,
I was a stick of butter
greasing 23rd Street
on my walk to work,
and this morning
I was treated to a
coming-attractions reel
for Fall of New York.

Out of Chaos

In the time before time,
while I swam the Tethys Sea,
and wandered the plains of Pangaea,
you were there, igneous and undefined.

Through the Laramide epoch,
Chronos, Chaos and tectonic slip
worked their orogenic magic,
and Gaia's labor gave birth to you.

Into the Cretaceous I watched,
as a deep slow subduction,
drove you, compelled you upward,
out of the plains and into my view.

I have crossed the alluvial sands,
and braved the ice of the Pleistocene,
to lie with you by the glow of caldera heat,
and be quenched by your glacial waters

Dance with me, 'round the ring of fire,
and explore the depths of Mariana.
Sit with me atop continental divides
until we are rendered, consumed again by Vulcan

La Cantera

I remember Friday night I drove
in circles, wasting rental gas, and
obsessively checking my watch.
Three hours from DC to San Antonio
plus the 5 months since you said goodbye.
I never told you how I cried and tried
to hate you, because when I saw you walk
through security 147 days dissolved,
like a sugar cube on my tongue.

And I remember Saturday night too,
after 18 holes, a delicate petite syrah
and two of the best damn steaks in Texas,
we laughed, drank XO and smoked Cohibas.
When you excused yourself for a moment,
every last man watched you catwalk out,
and then turned to me and said
"boy you're one lucky sombitch"
I just gave them a nod and a smile,
because they had no idea how lucky I was.

Insomnia

Sleep
as a desire
is gone,
reality
having surpassed
my dreams,
weariness
the price I pay
that I may
sense my joy
in full lucidity.

Dark hours crawl
begrudgingly
towards dawn,
I anticipate
our first
morning embrace.
If fitful dreams
invade the stillness,
I brush them
from your face.

Your love
quenches my heart,
slakes my soul,
far more
than the peace
of endless slumber.
I count myself
as blessed
and look forward
to years
of insomnia
with you.

Simplicity

Sunday morning sunlight
chases tiny rabbits
across the bedroom
and you are beautiful
in the shadows.
Blankets pulled overhead
keep Saturday night's toll
at bay for the moment
and you are enticing
in the goose down.
Newsprint smudged
fingers fetch you aspirin
with sparkling water back
and you are sexy
in the naked daylight.
I fell in love with you
on just such a morning,
3000 miles to the west
and you were beautiful
in the retreating fog.

Poet Warrior

I am the Norse god Bragi,
lyricist for the conquests
and defeats of antiquity.
I have sailed the North Sea
by aurora borealis light,
singing songs of victory
drunk with the spoils
of Lindesfarne Abbey.

I am a Celtic warrior born
from the waters of the Rhine
before stone sheathed steel.
With the blessings of Taranis
I have marched into battle
to taste Etruscan blood
and watch Virdomarus
fall to the sword of Rome.

I am of the tribe Myaamia
descended from ancient Adena.
I've hunted with wolven stealth
and flown on raven's wings.
I swear an oath of vengeance
to the Moon Earth and Sun;
the Ohio shall one day flow red
with the white man's blood.

The Weight of My Own Self Importance

How pretentious
the poet's pen is,
nattering nonsense
cobbled and collated
into couplets and quatrains.

The mysteries of life
explained; I am, in iamb.
A lot of alliteration;
love's loss lamented
line by line.

Pen and pad in hand
we toil and tarry 'til
the world weeps
in wonderment
at what we've written.

Sad Girl on an Uptown Train

It was just
another subway
Monday morning
as the city and I
shook off
the weekend.
The rustle
of newspaper
hide and seek
was muted
by MP3 players
and the steady click
of BlackBerry thumbs.

She wedged in
from the 28th Street
platform, wrapped
in wool and leather,
her hair tousled
by an unfair wind.
The sorrow she wore
did not go well
with Louis Vuitton
so I painted a smile
on her face with my eyes,
and loved her all the way
to 77th Street.

9 to 5 Icarus

These days King Minos
wears a suit and tie
and drives a new Bentley,
but he still has to deal
with the same bull,
rotten kids, bad wife;
fucking cow!

This is Manhattan,
not Knossos, so
there's no labyrinth here,
just subways tunnels
and skyscrapers,
but it can still be hard
to find a way out.

The wings of our fathers
come with warning labels
and we still ignore them
when we get high.
It's fortunate that this prison
only holds me from 9 to 5
and New Jersey
is a relatively short flight.

Eastern Terminus

The eastern terminus of the Lincoln
Highway is Times Square, New York,
New York; the confluence of Broadway,
Seventh Avenue and 42nd Street. Three
thousand three hundred and eighty nine
miles from San Francisco to the Cross-
roads of the World, cut through the
Rockies, across the broken heartland
and over the big shoulders. There is no
poetry here only clichéd mannequins, neon
buskers and Moriarty's ghost. Pale travelers,
blown in from Bountiful to Bedford, stand
on line at Bubba Gump and an old stripper
cries in the shadow of some forty odd stories.
Jesus used to ride the crystal ball but now we
Seek our salvation in the ticker's rise and fall;
God is dead after all. This is jazz, blues and
rock n roll, marquee lights and urine stained
sidewalks, the end of a long road, destiny
manifest and an innocent kiss at midnight.

Q&A
With Poet Steven Marty Grant

Q: You are lost in the desert, the situation is terminal, and the fates allow you a single word to leave behind to help others understand what your writing aimed to do-- what would that word be?

A: Such a tough question to answer. Like all writers I want my stuff to be all things, to all people but I know that is unreasonable. In the end I hope that people can connect with what I write so I am going with "Relatable".

Q: Of the pieces included in this volume, which is your favorite?

A: I don't even *like* a good number of them but I thought they were important because they showed my evolution as writer. Also I find when I re-read them I am transported right back to the time and place that inspired their creation. Some come from dark times that I don't necessarily want to revisit. Without a doubt I can say that "La Cantera" is my favorite from this collection.

Q: What inspired the piece?

A: When I met my wife, she was living in Washington DC and I was living in San Diego. We worked for the same company and met at a work function in DC. She was in a relationship as was I but we flirted anyway. We stayed in touch and both of us ended up single again and as coincidence would have were both going to another work function in New York. One thing leads to another and we started to date, long distance. After a few months she broke up with me to go back to the guy she had been dating when we first met. I was pretty fucked up over it because I was crazy about her but I knew enough to cut her off clean and make no contact. While we were apart I went to Europe and made sure that a mutual friend told her how much fun I had while I was there. Long story short, after several months she reinitiated contact and after some negotiation decided to meet me for a weekend in the middle. Honestly, when I planned the trip I was thinking I would nail her, fly home and we'd never talk again. The poem is a good summary of how the weekend turned out and we are coming up on our seventh anniversary so it has a happy continuing.

Q: How long have you been writing?
Was there a particular moment when you knew this was something you would pursue?

A: I started writing song lyrics with a band, just out of High School. Poetry was just the natural evolution of that, I guess. I was a drummer so I was never much of a song writer but I did okay as a lyricist.

I am not sure I have ever pursued writing so much as it has pursued me. When I was in college my writing professors all encouraged me to submit some of my early work (like "Search for Comparison") and some stuff was published. Since I left the cushy college life, writing is something that demands my time when I need to process emotion. If I am content I don't write much.

Q: You have a very distinctive style and voice.
Have you found the publishing world receptive?

A: In general I would say yes. I experiment with form and content and some of my stuff can get a little out there. I have a good support system of online writers that I trust and when I stray too far off reservation they pull me back. Because of that and my obsessive tinkering and rewriting, I get accepted by about 30% of the places I submit to.

Q: Please briefly discuss with us your creative process.
Do you outline ideas? What triggers generally act as inspiration for you?
How much time do you spend writing on a daily/weekly basis?

A: I tend to write from a single phrase or image and the piece develops from there. For example the poem "Out of Chaos" was written around the opening phrase "In the time before time". I liked the cadence of the line and it grew into a poem about the destiny of two people together. I got a little crazy with the geology metaphor but after many tweaks it turned out okay.

Scenes or emotion are my real triggers. A sad thought or something I might have seen on the subway that struck me. A poem like "Lost Forever" was written the night Bukowski died because I was just really down. I had only discovered him a few years before and then he was gone.

I try to write every morning before work for an hour or so. My day job is not exactly "creatively stimulating" so by the time I get home there is not much left to give the muse.

I write most things in straight blank verse, paragraph form, and then I let the content determine line and stanza breaks.

Q: Famous last words?

A: "Wait I wasn't finished!"

(*Drum roll…*)

Q: Most important question of them all: favorite curse word?

A: Sorry to be boring but it is really tough to beat "FUCK!"

The Folks Who Made It Happen

Steven Marty Grant is a hospitality sales professional living and working in New York City. A former journalist, musician and slacking underachiever, his poems have appeared in The Writer, The Ampersand (&) Review, The Melancholy Dane, Spring Harvest, VVC Drama & English Literary Journal, The Flask & Pen, Vivid Online, Sleep, Snort, Fuck and any web site with low enough standards to accept his work. Steven graduated from a school you've never heard of and had so many majors that even he is confused as to what his degree is in. He is married to a wonderful, patient woman and has the most perfect daughter any man could ask for.

Ruth Walters is a practicing attorney in the Pacific Northwest, where she lives with a phalanx of imaginary boyfriends who are much better behaved than any real ones. Ruth is an accomplished poet and essayist, and graduated University of Michigan Law School with honors in drinking sangria and editing academic journal articles until the wee hours.

Harmoni McGlothlin is an award winning screenwriter, a sometimes fiction writer, essayist and occasional poet who often prefers her delusions to reality. However she prefers wine to both delusions and reality. Harmoni's work has been honored with a Silver Telly Award, placed as a finalist at the International Page Awards, and has appeared in numerous publications. Her first volume of poetry, Venus Laughs, is also available through Grace Notes Books.

Harmoni is the founder of The Grace Notes Foundation, an organization supporting the literary arts through publishing and offering numerous resources for creative writers.

Visit www.GraceNotesBooks.Com
for more information about this author, The
Grace Notes Foundation, and Grace Notes Books.

Visit
www.GraceNotesBook.com

To check out our other great poetry, novel, and memoir titles as well as our print magazine *Notes*.

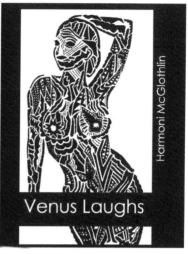

GN Publishing also offers an array of merchandise from t-shirts & apparel to coffee mugs, custom office supplies, and greeting cards. All GN products feature original artwork, ranging from beautiful surrealism to stylized modern pieces, combined with poignant & humorous quotes and/or poetry.

Writers! Visit NotesAndGraceNotes.com our online writing workshop!

Made in the USA
Charleston, SC
31 August 2011